Habitat and Land

Human Settlement Issues

Human Settlement Issues 1

HABITAT AND LAND

Len Gertler

Published in association with
The Centre for Human Settlements
at the University of British Columbia

1978

UNIVERSITY OF BRITISH COLUMBIA PRESS

VANCOUVER

HABITAT AND LAND

© The University of British Columbia 1978

Canadian Cataloguing in Publication Data

Gertler, L. O., 1923-
 Habitat and land
 (Human settlement series)
 Includes bibliographical references.

ISBN 0-7748-0100-X

 1. Land use — Planning. 2. Regional
planning. 3. City planning. 4. United
Nations Conference on Human Settlements,
Vancouver, B.C., 1976. I. University of
British Columbia. Centre for Human
Settlements. II. Title. III. Series.

HD111.G47   333.7 C78-002099-5

Printed in Canada by
MORRISS PRINTING COMPANY LTD.
Victoria, British Columbia

CONTENTS

ILLUSTRATIONS

1. Sub-standard Dwellings in Rio de Janeiro.
2. A Group of School Children in East Africa.
3. A View of the Ginza, the Main Shopping Thoroughfare of Tokyo.
4. A Congested City Street in the Old City of Delhi.
5. A Section of Singapore Which Shows the Contrast between Old and New Buildings.
6. A Street in a Poor Section of Calcutta.
7. A General View of the Jurong Industrial Estate in Singapore.
8. Toa Payoh Housing Estate on the Northern Outskirts of Singapore.

FOREWORD

The U.N. Conference on Human Settlements, Habitat '76, met in Vancouver during June 1976 and concluded with a Declaration of Principles as well as specific recommendations for national action and international co-operation. The conference was the culmination of a four-year process of substantive preparation and governmental consultations on a wide range of issues affecting human settlements.

In recognition of the global significance of these issues and the United Nations' initiative of convening a conference in Vancouver, the University of British Columbia established its Centre for Human Settlements. The centre's mandate includes continuity of research and dissemination of the issues underlying the Habitat Conference, highlighted by its many resolutions. The centre pursues its mandate through a programme of invitational seminars involving academics and professionals and attracting scholars-in-residence to spend varying amounts of time on the campus for research and teaching. Subsequently, the centre publishes the proceedings of the seminars and the work of its scholars-in-residence through the University of British Columbia Press, which generously agreed to initiate a continuing sequence under the general heading of Human Settlement Issues. It is our hope that the publication of scholarly work and seminar proceedings will materially assist in forwarding the work initiated by the U.N. conference and encourage governments and international organizations to pursue the resolutions adopted in Vancouver.

It is our pleasure to begin the series with the publication of *Habitat and Land* by Professor Leonard Gertler of the University of Waterloo. Professor Gertler is an established scholar who has worked for governments and taught several generations of students. He combines the realistic approach of the professional with the thoughtful analysis of the academic. His subject is central to all aspects of human settlements and is at the core of many of the Habitat resolutions. The preamble to these resolutions states:

Land, because of its unique nature and the crucial role it plays in human settlements, cannot be treated as an ordinary asset controlled by individuals and subject to the pressures and inefficiency of the market — . Governments must have the political will to evolve and implement innovative and adequate urban and rural land policies as a cornerstone of the efforts to improve the quality of life in human settlements.

It is in this context that it is appropriate to initiate the series on human settlement issues by the publication of its first volume *Habitat and Land*.

H. PETER OBERLANDER
Director
Centre for Human Settlements

PREFACE

This study by Professor Leonard Gertler provides an important contribution to what must inevitably become a sharper debate on urban land policy in Canada. The debate will be many-faceted, covering environmental, social, economic, and jurisdictional issues. It will be fueled by many competing demands: to preserve agricultural land, to protect environmentally sensitive areas, to maintain aesthetic resources, to increase equity, to conserve energy, to curb sprawl, to limit land monopolies, to return land profits to the public sector, and, on the other side, to free the urban land market from constraints.

All of these problems have been the subject of considerable study, and the resulting extensive literature attests to diverse viewpoints and perceptions. These problems have also stirred government responses around the world expressed in equally diverse urban land policies and programmes.

In *Habitat and Land*, Professor Gertler provides an analytical framework and synthesis for understanding and comparing urban land policies internationally. He then applies that framework to the policies of three groups of countries. The first, the United Kingdom, the United States, and France, are closely tied to Canada. The second, Australia, India, and Singapore, are Commonwealth countries with similar government and legal traditions. The third, Sweden, Denmark, and The Netherlands, are western European social democracies that have had experiences we should not ignore in the process of finding our own way.

Most of Professor Gertler's data comes from Habitat, the 1976 Vancouver United Nations Conference that tried to raise world consciousness of possible solutions to several human settlement problems.

For the people of the Third World, it was a global endeavour to understand what governments could do about squatter settlements or totally inadequate water supplies for the great mass of humanity living in rural villages. But for most Canadians, apart from heightening our understanding of world conditions and our international obligation to reduce disparity, the conference was an opportunity to share knowledge and experience. Gertler takes up that opportunity.

The conference also succeeded in obtaining international consensus on a charter for national actions to improve human settlements. The section of that charter on land policy is Gertler's starting point. It was among the most contentious subjects at the conference and was the principal subject of debate within the Canadian delegation.

What *Habitat and Land* shows by inference is that the public debate in Canada so far has been very shallow. The international experience provides by comparison a rich repertoire of policy instruments unique to each country. Its analysis here by *scope, form,* and *value orientation* gives us much food for thought. The fact that it was written in Vancouver, the site of the conference, where the intense pressure of urbanization on a very limited land resource is more extreme than anywhere else in Canada, lends urgency to the need for both further thought and action.

The School of Community and Regional Planning at the University of British Columbia is pleased to be associated with this endeavour.

BRAHM WIESMAN
Director
School of Community and Regional Planning

ACKNOWLEDGMENTS

The project associated with this study owes much to the research assistance of Paul St. Pierre; to the administrative support of Gerald Savory and Morfudd Jackson; to those graduate students and faculty at the School of Community and Regional Planning, U.B.C., who offered stimulating discussion and information; to Brahm Wiesman, co-sponsor on behalf of his school, who sustained a deep interest in the exploration throughout my sojourn at U.B.C.; to Robin Fried, Director, Community and Regional Planning, Centre for Continuing Education, who generously made available Habitat Committee notes and files on the Habitat Forum; and, certainly not least, to Peter Oberlander, Director of the Centre for Human Settlements, who expressed the need for a treatment of land policy in terms of the issues raised at Habitat, and who graciously invited me to take that on.

LG

Habitat and Land

I

SCOPE OF LAND POLICY CONCERNS

N·B

"Land, because of its unique nature and the crucial role it plays in human settlements, cannot be treated as an ordinary asset, controlled by individuals and subject to the pressures and inefficiencies of the market.... Public control of land use is ... indispensable to its protection as an asset and the achievement of the long-term objectives of human settlement policies and strategies." These are the words that heralded an unprecedented global happening: the approval by 131 nations participating in the United Nations Conference on Human Settlements (Habitat) of seven land policy "recommendations for national action."[1]

The themes and summary statements of these recommendations were as follows:

1 *Land resource management:* Land is a scarce resource whose management should be subject to public surveillance or control in the interest of the nation.

2 *Control of land use changes:* Change in the use of land, especially from agricultural to urban, should be subject to public control and regulation.

3 *Recapturing plus value:* The unearned increment resulting from the rise in land values resulting from change in use of land, from public investment or decision or due to the general growth of the community must be subject to appropriate recapture by public bodies (the community), unless the situation calls for other additional measures such as new patterns of ownership, the general acquisition of land by public bodies.

4 *Public ownership:* Public ownership, transitional or permanent, should be used, wherever appropriate, to secure and control areas of urban expansion and protection; and to implement urban and rural land reform processes, and supply serviced land at price levels which can secure socially acceptable patterns of development.

5 *Patterns of ownership:* Past patterns of ownership rights should be transformed to match the changing needs of society and be collectively beneficial.

3

6 *Increase in usable land:* The supply of usable land should be maintained by all appropriate methods including soil conservation, control of desertification and salination, prevention of pollution, and use of land capability analysis and increased by long-term programmes of land reclamation and preservation.

7 *Information needs:* Comprehensive information on land capability, characteristics, tenure, use and legislation should be collected and constantly up-dated so that all citizens and levels of government can be guided as to the most beneficial land use allocations and control measures.[2]

Since these recommendations will serve as a framework for a comparative interpretation of land policies in a group of selected countries, the approved text is reproduced in full in the appendix. It is of utmost importance to their value as discussion themes to understand that these are not bland, perfunctory statements, but in fact one of the major outcomes of a two-year U.N. preparatory process, and of intense, albeit kid-gloved, ideological in-fighting at the Habitat Conference itself. Generalization, one of the inescapable conventions of large conferences, should not be confused with policy impotence. Sometimes the "fencing" took the form of outright disagreement between countries, for example, when New Zealand in committee declared that it could not support the recommendation on land values in its original sweeping version — emphasis should be on the recapture of "speculative elements of incremental value" exclusively — and Finland followed with an assertion of unqualified support for the land recommendations.[3]

At other times the struggle for policy positions was reflected within national delegations, as typified by the acrobatics of the Canadian delegation on this same issue: the recapture of plus value. Peter Nicholson, a member of the Canadian Participation Secretariat and an adviser to the Canadian Habitat Delegation, has provided a vivid account of the evolution of the Canadian stance. In a single debate, Canada moved from the sponsorship of an amendment which suggested something less than a 100 per cent appropriation of the plus value (the incriminating phrase was "an equitable portion of") to the statement which became the final formulation of the text (item 3, above). This incorporated a drafting group's term "unearned increment," but rejected the group's confinement of the action to "urban and suburban" land. Instead, the more general reference, "change in use of land," was employed, and a new concept introduced: "appropriate recapture." "To those who under political pressure reluctantly abandoned 'an equitable portion'," Nicholson states, "this notion of 'appropriate recapture' reintroduces sufficient ambiguity to argue a status quo position at home."[4]

From Canada's point of view these gyrations were not capricious, but reflected divergent philosophical views within the delegation, views which were urged on the delegates from the wings, from the Habitat Forum where the Canadian Real Estate Association declared that "market forces must remain dominant" and "government intervention should be limited to what is required to make the market work better";[5] and where, in dramatic contrast, the Citizens Association to Save the Environment inveighed against "land investment for profit," and the Students of the Interprovincial Seminar of the United Nations stressed that "at this Habitat Conference, Canada must support the resolution regarding the return of plus-values of land to the communities in whose boundaries that land lies."[6] The land recommendations were, and are, a battleground.

Viewed synoptically, the seven land recommendations are very broad. They can be construed to encompass both the issues associated with urbanization as well as the agrarian concerns associated with "land reform." While each of these has a legitimate claim upon the policy-maker, this study, because it is written with a Canadian perspective, stresses the urban-related aspects.

The nature of the Canadian concern with land policy is suggested by the Habitat National Report, *Human Settlement in Canada*. Land, along with housing, is identified as one of "two key issues." This breaks down into worry about "sprawl," a settlement pattern which because of its low density and/or messy design is wasteful of land; about the conversion of productive agricultural land to urban uses — "good farmland cannot hold its own in an unregulated market"; about speculation — "the main problem . . . is the large unearned or 'windfall' profits that it can bring from the sale of land made valuable by *public* investments or decision"; and about "the high cost of land for urban development."[7]

The linking, in the public mind, of the cost of land with the escalating price of housing led to the announcement late in 1976 of a Federal/ Provincial Task Force on the Supply and Price of Serviced Residential Land. In this, and many other ways, land policy remains a lively public issue in Canada.

These Canadian antecedents are mentioned because they are the basis for my approach to both the Habitat recommendations, as already indi-cated, and to the selection of countries for comparative study. They are nation states that, by virtue of certain shared conditions, address those categories of land problems experienced by Canada. By proceeding in this manner, I hope to minimize the hazards in an international study (in other contexts, a blessing) of cultural diversity: drawing inferences for one place from fundamentally different environments. This, in fact, is one of the lessons of Habitat, where in the land discussions, such countries as Lesotho and Fiji were constrained to observe that the public (viz. "state") ownership of land would be a retrograde step wherever, as in these cases, the land was communally owned by the whole people.[8]

Three sets of countries will be examined: (1) the United Kingdom, the United States, and France, traditionally the countries most closely linked with the development of Canada; (2) Australia, India, and Singapore, a diverse group which because of their association with the British Commonwealth share with other members certain value systems, government, institutions, and legal traditions; (3) Sweden, Denmark, and The Netherlands, west European social democracies, which through cultural and economic relationships have become increasingly part of our cognitive world.

An effort will be made to treat each country in the first group concisely, searching for the inner logic and rationale of policy stances, while commenting on associated countries comparatively as the analysis proceeds. A concluding overview will be attempted. The other two groups of countries will be examined more synoptically with a view to highlighting those initiatives that make a unique contribution to the repertoire of land policies. The term "policy" in all cases will be understood to include objectives, strategies, and institutions.

This statement attempts to go beyond mere description in the presentation of national policies on land. An analytical framework is offered at the conclusion of Chapter 2 that assesses each country's position on the Habitat land issues in terms of the scope, form, and value orientation of policies. Thus a comparative, synoptic, evaluative view is afforded which, while not in itself the basis for critical judgment, permits the reader to judge the situation independently. The major information base, however, remains the official documents submitted to the Habitat conference.

2

DOMINANT INFLUENCES:
THE TRADITIONAL THREE

Land policy in the United Kingdom is viewed as an integral part of a comprehensive planning system. The "public surveillance" called for in recommendation no. 1 and the "control of land use changes" in recommendation no. 2 are built into a hierarchical system extending from strategic plans for the major regions of the country, such as the south-east and the north-west, to structural plans for the counties and local plans for the constituent districts. This planning system has a strong statutory base in the Town and Country Planning Act, 1947, and may be presumed to be effective in its allocative function with respect to land, with variations in performance in response to the ebb and flow of political influences.

The British approach seems to combine a comprehensive strategy, supplemented by quite bold intervention in key problem areas, with a strong penchant for institutional reform. Thus under the general planning powers of the country it has been possible to designate green belts around major cities to define the limits of urban growth; to protect "heritage coasts," for example, in Scotland in the areas of North Sea oil exploration; and to preserve some 3,000 "conservation areas" which are selected areas — buildings, monuments, and their sites — of special architectural or historic interest.[1]

These regulatory powers for land management and use are complemented by the provisions of the National Parks and Access to the Countryside Act, 1949, which empowers its implementing agency, the Countryside Commission, to designate national parks, areas of outstanding natural beauty, and sites of special scientific interest for their plant or animal communities or geological features. The areas identified in this manner (and they are extensive; for example, national parks constitute nine per cent of the land area of England and Wales) are conserved and made accessible to the public without the public acquisition of the land. They

become subject to a land-use policy, under the general operation of the
Planning Act, that allows only those uses, essentially rural, which are
compatible with a national park function.[2]

The most important form of direct intervention to influence the national
settlement patterns in the British system, and with this the allocation of
land, is the authority to initiate new urban development under the New
Towns Act, 1946. The new towns programme is interpreted as "a syste-
matic attempt to alleviate some of the problems left by too fast a rate of
past urbanization and, in the process, to achieve a more efficient national
and regional distribution of population and employment and a better
quality of life."[3]

The British approach to new town development is distinguished by four
major features: public sector leadership; a comprehensive planning
process, integrating salient physical, social, and economic considerations;
special agencies designed for effective new town planning and implementation; and statutory land assembly and acquisition powers for development purposes.[4]

The land provisions are critical to the effectiveness of the new towns
programme and of general interest as a demonstration of how land can
be used creatively for positive community building. The development
corporation, the chosen agency for each town, is empowered to acquire
the land, by compulsory purchase if necessary, and in such a way that
inflated costs are avoided. The legislation provides for acquisition at
"existing use value" both for the original assembly and for subsequent
extensions. Accordingly, through the public ownership and control of
land, and its initial capitalization at pre-existing values, land becomes the
key both to positive planning — the orderly, economic, and (if the fates
smile) inspired development of the town — and its ultimate financial
solvency. Proceeds from the recapture of "development value" as the
community grows (primarily through the terms of leases) go towards the
development costs of the town.[5]

This British experience is important because its operational validity has
been demonstrated over a period of thirty years in the development of
thirty-three new towns with an aggregate population of two million. And
now it has become the basis for a major initiative in general land policy,
the Community Land Act, 1975, which extends the "positive planning"
features of the new towns programme to the country as a whole.

The new comprehensive legislation together with its companion piece,
the Development Land Tax Bill, 1976, are designed to harness the
"recapturing of plus value" (Habitat land recommendation 3) and the
"public ownership of land" (recommendation 4) in the service of sound
and equitable development. Under an umbrella policy which will even-

tually require all local authorities to create public land banks "for private development up to a maximum of 10 years ahead," they have been given wide powers to buy, manage, and dispose of land under carefully defined terms. In these arrangements, the "unearned increment" in the terms defined by the Habitat recommendation will be retained by the "community" in two ways: by the statutory terms of public purchase, which will not exceed a level of twenty per cent above current use value; and by the disposal of public lands earmarked for industrial and commercial purposes on a leasehold basis only, with provision for the periodic renegotiation and renewal of leases to reflect and obtain the benefits of rising values. Individuals are able to obtain residential land on a freehold basis for private homes, but through a licensing arrangement with housebuilders that would foreclose opportunities of speculative profits on the land.[6]

The same policy objectives will be involved for private land transactions — eighty per cent of plus value will be appropriated by a development land tax. These new initiatives altogether are expected to yield substantial financial benefits for the public purse, by lower land prices for schools, public housing, open space, etc., and by the deployment of tax revenues between the central government and local authorities.[7] Whether they will be able to overcome the congenital difficulties of earlier generations of similar British policy — the "locking in" of land by recalcitrant owners or the real inflationary effects of "under the table" payments in private transactions — must be left to the adjudication of unfolding events.[8] Similarly, the effort to transfer the "formula" for successful land development and management from the limited scale of the new towns to the national scene remains largely untested.[9]

With regard to the fifth Habitat recommendation, "patterns of ownership," the British scene does not present any dramatic initiatives. It is a good example of how a liberal democratic society in response to social change gradually, and sometimes imperceptibly, alters the meaning and effect of basic concepts and institutions such as property and ownership. Notwithstanding the abortive attempt through the 1947 Town and Country Act to legislate what was really an ideological shift, the appropriation of development rights by the state, the patterns of land ownership reflect an evolutionary process of change. Public ownership has been extended, by legislation, from very specific public purposes such as roads, parks, and utilities, to land for general development. The rights of freehold land are qualified by the land development tax, by the state's power of compulsory acquisition, by the control of its price in public purchases, and generally by the reverberations of the planning system on its use. In this regard, the British concept of national parks — public access to and enjoyment of freehold landscape — suggests that the British have a more generous view of the public interest in private land than their North American cousins.

Institutional ownership in Britain is the third major component of the country's patterns of land tenure. The National Trust, a late Victorian voluntary institution, has become the custodian of over two hundred historic buildings and sites; and the Civic Trust concentrates on the conservation and enhancement of selective urban features, such as a Guildhall in Poole, Dorset, or the rehabilitation of a group of derelict early nineteenth-century houses in Lambeth, London.[10] This type of voluntary initiative on a national scale is one of the unique qualities of the British experience.

While the British appear to have systematically strengthened the control of land in the public interest, formal public policy does not entirely express the realities of the land market. Periodic explosions in land prices and the numerous shifts of the policy pendulum over the last thirty years are symptoms of underlying stress.

With respect to Habitat land recommendation 6, "increase in usable land," the major effort in Britain has been in the reclamation of industrially derelict land — the eyesores left by slag heaps and open-pit mines. The policy moves in two directions: the provision of grants to local authorities to eradicate the sins of the past; and the building-in of a legally enforceable requirement to carry out restoration as a condition of development consent to new undertakings.[11]

The consolidation after 1972 of planning, housing, and environmental functions into a single omnibus Ministry of the Environment has created a unique opportunity for rationalizing land information for technical and administrative purposes, and for the edification of the public. While sophistication in concepts and hardware is present, I gained the impression during a Canada-U.K. Consultation in December 1975 that Britain, like most countries, had a long way to go towards meeting information needs (recommendation 7) as defined by Habitat: "The establishment of a comprehensive information system involving all levels of government; and accessible to the public."

UNITED STATES

American land policy, viewed nationally, lacks the comprehensiveness of the British approach, relies more heavily on regulatory measures than on direct action, and has a decidedly experimental bent, particularly in the fiscal area, in contrast to Britain's commitment to far-reaching reforms.

In the broad fields of "land resource management" and "control of land use change" most of the action has been at state and local levels. Federal policy has been supportive, or stimulative, taking the form of

TABLE 1

City-Enacted Land-Use Controls, by Population Size of City and Other Characteristics

	No. of respondents	Architectural appearance[1]		Flood plain zoning		Growth limitation		Historical preservation		Marshland		Open space zoning		Instaln of public facilities[2]		Dedic. of land for pub. purp.[3]		Zng to protect natrl resources[4]	
	(A)	No.	%(A)	No.	%(A)	No.	%(A)	No.	%(A)	No.	%(A)	No.	%(A)	No.	%(A)	No.	%(A)	No.	%(A)
Total, all cities	1115	297	27	507	45	258	23	262	23	132	12	531	48	921	83	519	47	390	35
Population group																			
Over 500,000	10	3	30	5	50	2	20	8	80	2	20	6	60	8	80	4	40	2	20
250,000-500,000	18	4	22	12	67	1	6	9	50	4	22	7	38	14	78	8	44	1	6
100,000-250,000	61	15	25	33	54	14	23	30	49	11	18	23	38	51	83	33	54	17	28
50,000-100,000	142	43	30	61	43	38	27	37	27	16	11	70	49	127	89	75	53	51	36
25,000-50,000	282	71	25	131	46	66	23	62	22	30	11	142	50	226	80	128	45	99	35
10,000-25,000	602	161	27	265	44	137	23	116	19	69	11	283	47	495	82	271	45	220	37
Geographic region																			
North-east	252	58	23	130	52	74	29	72	29	61	24	119	47	189	75	101	40	91	36
North central	327	84	26	163	50	56	17	69	21	36	11	163	50	264	81	162	50	112	34
South	274	46	17	121	44	62	23	61	22	17	6	114	42	232	85	99	36	89	32
West	262	109	42	93	35	66	25	60	23	18	7	135	52	236	90	157	60	98	37
Metro/city type																			
Central	195	41	21	89	46	37	19	75	38	23	12	78	40	169	87	84	43	50	26
Suburban	592	206	35	285	48	170	29	114	19	81	14	302	51	481	81	297	50	220	37
Independent	328	50	15	133	41	51	16	73	22	28	9	151	46	271	83	138	42	120	37
Form of government																			
Mayor-council	279	72	26	123	44	65	23	73	26	35	13	141	51	213	76	124	44	99	35
Council-manager	769	214	28	348	45	180	23	171	22	75	10	360	47	664	86	366	48	266	35
Other	67	11	16	36	54	13	19	18	27	22	33	30	45	44	66	29	43	25	37

[1] Regulates aesthetic element of the environment.

[2] Requires installation of public facilities (such as sewers) by developers.

[3] Requires dedication of land for public purposes (such as schools and parks) by developers.

[4] Protects natural resources or ecological systems.

Source: U.S. Environmental Protection Agency, Environmental Management and Local Government, 1974.

mandatory state and local planning as a condition of financial assistance.

The onus of responsibility for land use planning, on a day-to-day basis, is assumed by municipalities, counties, and regional councils, operating under the authority of state "zoning and enabling acts."[12]

In addition to conventional controls, built around zoning and subdivision regulations, there has been considerable experiment at the local government level — city, suburban, metropolitan — with a number of special measures. These encompass nine types of action, including initiatives addressed directly to growth limitation, open space zoning, and the protection of natural resources and ecological systems (Table 1). The measures employed are either general in scope, such as development timing ordinances and growth ceilings, or involve the tactical manipulation of development rights and tax powers. The objective seems to be to discover a judicious mix of deterrents and incentives.[13]

The overview prepared by the U.S. Environmental Protection Agency shown in Table I indicates the relative importance of the different forms of land-use control, in terms of population size groups, region, and urban type. None of the approaches are in effect in more than half of the 1,115 cities over 10,000 in population. There are five types of control that relate most closely to the general Habitat recommendations (1 and 2); and the percentages of the cities using them are as follows: flood plain zoning, 45 per cent; growth limitation, 23 per cent; historical preservation, 23 per cent; open space zoning, 48 per cent; zoning to protect natural resources, 35 per cent. Some of the emphases that emerge are of interest: flood plain zoning gets almost equal attention in central and suburban cities; growth limitation measures are used most in suburban areas (29 per cent); there is a conspicuous interest in historical preservation in the largest places, in the north-east region and in the centre of cities; open space zoning is strongest in the top size group (over 500,000); and zoning to protect natural resources is most common in the smaller cities, ranging from 10,000 to 100,000 people, and in suburban and "independent" cities.[14]

Comprehensive land-use planning at the state level is the exception rather than the rule. Only about twelve states, randomly located across the country with some bias to the midwest and New England, combine broad policies with land-use regulation systems.[15] The rest have pursued a more incremental approach. Land use programmes that are applied in half or more of the fifty states are the following, in order of frequency:

Differential assessment laws: tax measures designed to give property tax relief to owners of agricultural or open space land. These include three types: preferential assessment — assessment based on existing use-value; deferred taxation — assessment based on existing use-value plus the requirement of a payment of back taxes if the land is converted to an urban use; and restricted agreements — assessment at existing use-value, reinforced by a state-owner contract committing the owner to the payment of back taxes on violation of the agreement.

Surface mining: the regulation of surface mines, such as sand, gravel, and stone, by state rules and regulations, or by technical guidelines.

Power plant siting: the location of power plants and related facilities.

Coastal zone management: state participation in the coastal zone management programmes authorized by the Coastal Zone Management Act, 1972, which provides grants to states undertaking "programs for the beneficial use and protection of the lands and waters of the coastal zones," i.e., the Pacific, Atlantic, and Great Lakes shorelines.

Flood plain management: the regulation of land use and building in the floodplains of the state territory.[16]

The U.S. National Report to Habitat is refreshingly candid about the overall effectiveness of the foregoing local and state initiatives. Reference is made to the "inherent limitations" of municipal planning. "Among these limitations are the regulators' inflexibility, their proscriptive rather than prescriptive character, and their general ability to shape a highly efficient and amenable living environment. The results are indelibly recorded for all to see in the contemporary urban and suburban city-scape."[17] And the sober judgments on efforts at the state level is that "land use planning is by and large a fragmented assortment of functions carried on at several levels of government with little interagency or inter-governmental coordination."[18]

Against this background of worry about the ongoing mechanism, the issue of a "national land use planning bill" has surfaced in Congress throughout the seventies (1973-76), but none of the competing legislative proposals have been able to carry the support of both houses. This type of initiative which, it is confidently predicted, "will undoubtedly resurface in Congress, if not this year then the next," would lift the regulatory approach of the most planning-conscious states to the national level. Target concerns are the control of land use around major facilities, the consistency of local programmes with state plans, the impact of large-scale private projects, and the protection of flood plains, fault zones, and critical environments generally.[19]

In a manner which appears characteristic of the pragmatic American approach — do but do avoid ideological confrontation — some of the important objectives of the proposed land-use bills are being implemented indirectly, through federal legislation setting pre-conditions for the enjoyment of benefits. Perhaps the most far-reaching in effect is the Housing and Community Development Act, 1974, which requires that recipients of assistance for housing (moderate- and low-income) shall establish by the summer of 1977 a comprehensive planning process, placing residential development in a total land use and environmental context. This is but one of a large number of acts, in the areas of health, transportation, environmental protection, rural development, etc. which appear to work in the same direction. Planning by leverage is reported to be having some success, but the approach would seem to run the risk of perverse effects: conflicting and/or overlapping objectives, strategies, and organizations.[20]

Potential for more direct federal action on the national growth pattern is implied by the Urban Growth and New Communities Act, 1970. Its operating mechanisms, however, are very different from the British (and for that matter European) counterpart, which is perceived as an instrument of national policy. The approach is tactical if not fragmentary: fiscal and experimental. Its basic device is a federal guarantee of the developer's capital debt incurred for the heavy "front-end investment" in land and utilities. Public assembly and ownership of land within a framework of explicit development policies, the sine qua non of new community programmes in Britain and the west European social democracies, have no place in the American policy repertoire.[21]

The struggle against land speculation and profits has been one of the perennial myths of American life and politics, from Lincoln Steffens and *The Shame of the Cities* at the turn of the century to Ralph Nader and his contemporary report on *Power and Land in California*. Surprisingly, however, public policy shows little preoccupation with the recapture of the "unearned increment" in land values (Habitat land recommendation 3). It is possible that the capital gains tax has taken some of the steam out of this issue.

While public ownership of land as a management and control device is rare, American courts lean increasingly towards a liberal interpretation of "eminent domain," the acquisition of land, by expropriation if necessary, by public agencies. It is reported that such purposes as "elimination of urban sprawl, irrational growth patterns, and inefficient use of land" have become acceptable as valid public uses for the exercise of eminent domain. Nevertheless, land use programmes at all government levels are still mainly confined to the traditional public purposes for land acquisition: schools, parks, roads, etc. It follows that in the developed regions of the country the "patterns of ownership" do not deviate significantly from a certain predominant mould: a privately possessed landscape, breached only for those limited public purposes that are sanctioned by long practice. While changing needs and pressures have given rise to new approaches — such as transfer of development rights and bonus and incentive systems — these methods are "rarely applied."[22]

It is well known that the collection, processing, and analysis of physical environmental data, including land information, has attained a high level of sophistication in the United States. Whether this has been co-ordinated and organized in a manner that provides consistently and comprehensively the information required both for sound policies and intelligent public response is doubtful. One of the more promising developments in recent years has been the emergence at the local government level of urban growth management systems, "designed to control or influence the rate, amount, or geographic pattern of growth." These involve the integration into a single system of a number of conventional elements: legislation, administrative techniques, planning processes, and fiscal measures. And it is presumed that the total will be greater than the sum of its parts; there will be an enhanced capability arising from the more effective mobilization and deployment of government resources.[23]

Information flowing between the various components is the essential lubricant of the entire system. A recent evaluation of the management system approach, based on thirteen case studies, indicates that the information correlative is not at present well developed. Research on the impact of land-use controls is very limited, with unfortunate consequences for policy. "The choice for communities," it is reported, "is either to delay action until exploratory research can be completed or to proceed and monitor for desired and undesired effects and alter the controls as experience is gained. The first tactic is politically impractical in most instances, but the second tactic is generally ignored. . . . No body of knowledge or insight is being recorded for future use by the operating agencies themselves, and no comparative evaluations across systems have been made."[24]

At this stage the most positive aspect of this management approach, from the point of view of the Habitat concern with "public access" (land recommendation 7), is the provision in such systems of "informal entry points." These are places in the administration where the concerned citizen or actor in the development process can obtain in a single contact whatever information the systems can yield, and "under circumstances that are not binding to either side."[25]

Land policy in France presents a strikingly different picture from the American scene. In contrast to a loose, permissive, experimental approach, French policy is highly structured. It is conditioned by a broad planning framework, with economic, environmental, and urban dimensions, which takes the form of a centrally guided but regionally oriented administrative structure, and a number of major development concepts.

Policies for the management and use of land, the general concerns of the Habitat recommendations, make most sense when they are seen in the general setting of the French planning system, which has the following features:

— a series of four-year national plans: economic and indicative.

— twenty-one programme regions, substantial "natural" subdivisions of the country like Normandie (Haute et Basse), Centre: the Paris basin, Bourgogne, and Cote d'Azur, mandated to prepare master plans and implement regional development programmes by the co-ordination of the relevant departments.

— a central planning agency to co-ordinate the involvement of central government departments in regional programmes. This is the Délégation à l'Aménagement du Territoire et à l'Action Régionale (DATAR: Delegations for Regional Planning Development and Action).

— two local planning instruments, applied at the level of the commune: one conceptual and the other legal and administrative. These are *Schéma Directeur d'Aménagement Urbain* (SDAU), i.e., Structure Plans for Urban Development; and Plan d'Occupation des Sols (POS), i.e., Detailed Land Use Plan. The 1967 Planning Law requires that communes with populations of 50,000 or more submit both structure and land use plans to the Ministry of Public Works and Housing.

— a national settlement policy featuring
   (a)   containment of the growth of Paris, and
   (b)   the channelling of Parisian-based growth into five new towns within the Paris basin.
   (c)   the fostering of metropolitan counter-magnets: in the north — Lille, Roubaux, Tourcoing; north-east — Metz, Nancy and Strasbourg; south-east — Lyon, Saint-Etienne, Grenoble; north-west — Nantes; south-west — Bordeaux; and south — Toulouse and Marseille.
   (d)   promotion of middle-sized towns, in the 20,000 to 100,000 population range, with emphasis on quality of life ("un urbanisme aux dimensions humaines").
   (e)   the restraining of the rural population exodus by the encouragement of a process of self-help and improvement ("dans une structure de coopération intercommunale") in country towns, typically places of five to fifteen thousand people and their service areas.

— a national system of parks and open spaces consisting of national and regional parks; nature reserves; special places of historic or scenic interest; and green spaces, developed in and around urban regions for environmental purposes ("constituent les éléments de regéneration du milieu"), and

— a mechanism for directly shaping the settlement pattern by the planning and development of new towns. The mechanism is the Groupe des Villes Nouvelles (Central New Towns Group) which administers the financial and general planning aspects of the programme, and the community planning syndicates (syndicats communautaires d'aménagement) for each of the nine new towns presently being created.[26]

Land policy in France can be viewed as an integral part of the foregoing planning and development system: the means for reserving, controlling, and acquiring land, at reasonable cost, which is essential for carrying out both structural (SDUA) and land use (POS) plans. From another perspective, the distinctive substance and style of French policy can best be understood as an approach that has evolved out of a positive interventionist stance. This interpretive view has been stressed in a recent study:

With the rapid development of public planning involving major urban development and infrastructural projects, it became apparent very quickly that something more than the preparation of land use plans and the traditional means of manipulating the development process through taxation or zoning was required. Fears were expressed over increases in land prices created as a consequence of planning decisions. Such increases not only helped thwart the planning process itself, but also made the public works components of this process very costly.[27]

Responding to the tough and demanding criteria demonstrated by this kind of experience, a number of instruments were designed to overcome the land market constraints on public policy. These are known as Zone d'Aménagement Différé (ZAD: Zone of Deferred Planning) and Zone d'Aménagement Concerté (ZAC: Zone of Concerted Planning), the "cornerstones" of a programme launched in 1962. The "zones" referred to are areas that may be designated by municipalities, regional prefects, or by ministerial decree, in accordance with their varying purposes. Within a ZAD, the state, or its delegated agent, can exercise a preemptive right of purchase on real estate entering the market, for a specified period of time at a specified price, usually the market value at the time of designation. A ZAC is an area that may be designated, after preemptive acquisition, on public lands for the purpose of defining the land services: drainage, utilities, roads, etc., which, with some exceptions, are the responsibility of private developers.[28]

Broadly speaking, ZAD becomes a vehicle for capturing the betterment value (unearned increment) resulting from public investment and for the strategic extension of public land ownership. These two Habitat concerns are the nub of French land policy. ZAD can be orchestrated towards these purposes in a variety of ways. It may be used as an anti-speculative device for a period of three years (provisory ZAD) by holding the line on land prices and allowing planning studies to proceed "without prejudicial haste." It may prevent the private appropriation of the betterment value around major public projects, such as highways and new town developments, before, during, and after construction, indeed up to a maximum period of fourteen years (structural and definitive ZAD). And ZAD (definitive) may be used more positively to assemble land, for immediate and long-range needs, for more specific public purposes, such as land banking to assure the orderly extension of towns and cities, for open space networks in the rural-urban fringe, or for the sites of new towns. This power is made operational for municipalities exercising the right of pre-emption by a central government programme that provides loan capital for strategic land acquisition.[29]

The ZAD programme has been very active. By 1974 it covered over 400,000 hectares, of which about one-third were in the Paris region. It has served impressively as a monitor of regional land markets, since the regional prefect must receive notice of any intended voluntary property transfers within a ZAD by a Déclaration d'Intention d'Aliéner (DIA: Declaration of Intent to Transfer Title). In Paris alone, some 24,000 DIAs were received during twelve years of operation. This represents a level of land market direction that has eluded most countries.[30]

The "deferred planning" approach has some important repercussions on patterns of ownership, and the relationships between state and property. There is a manifest attempt to steer a middle course between public purposes and the rights of the private landowner. The pre-emptor has sufficient time after notification to take action, but not unlimited time, not more than three months. The pre-emptor may reject the vendor's price and instead base compensation on an evaluation by the property assessment service. But if the owner is not happy with the offer he may request an arbitrated price established by the court that customarily adjudicates expropriation cases. Even this is not immediately binding; for a period of two months after the court's decision both the owner and the pre-emptor may withdraw from the transactions.

Nor does all the initiative rest with the public sector pre-emptor. One year after the application for a ZAD, a landowner may request the pre-emptor to acquire his land either at an agreed or arbitrated price. If the offer is rejected, or the pre-emptor does not respond within six months, the property in question is thereafter exempted from pre-emption. If the offer is accepted by the pre-emptor, it is binding; the owner cannot withdraw his request. The balance of rights is delicate, some would say precarious.[31]

The innovative nature of French land policy, and its direct assault on problems experienced by many countries, provokes critical interest in its effectiveness. It is difficult to assess its national impact on the basis of the aggregative information available such as the observation that 1/100th of the national territory is covered by the ZAD. Much more needs to be known about its regional impact. Some evaluations that have been made are in some respects contradictory. A World Bank study, published in 1974, emphasizes the difficulties, principally that the ZAD policy has not been able to check the escalation of the general level of urban land prices. It is, however, not at all clear that this was ever a declared policy objective.[32]

On the other hand, a Canadian study, published in 1976, reports substantial progress, mainly on the basis of an in-depth study in the region of Paris. The major advantages for the ZAD are the creation of an umbrella under which planning for certain critical areas, freed from land price pressures, could proceed without disruptive haste; the acquisition of land for development at prices substantially below market prices in non-ZAD areas, in fact, at an average level of about one-fifth to one-half the prevailing level; the pre-emption of betterment arising from public investment; and, not least, the attainment of all the foregoing benefits without freezing the land market or stomping too heavily on landowners.[33]

OVERVIEW

It is apparent that the three countries examined have made quite distinctive policy responses to problems that they have in common. To place these differences in perspective I have summarized and compared the policy stances of each country with respect to three major issues and three dimensions of policy as shown in Table 2. The themes of the seven Habitat recommendations are reduced to three generic issues: use, which includes all that is encompassed by the "management" and "control of land use" themes as well as soil conservation and capability aspects of recommendation 7; cost, which refers to the general concern with land price and cost, taxation, and the "recapture of plus value"; and ownership, which relates to the substance of both recommendations 4 and 5, "public ownership" and "patterns of ownership." The reclamation aspects of "increase in usable land" are not included in the summary, since the physical environmental conditions affecting this issue vary so much from country to country. "Information needs" is not included because, ironically, the Habitat material does not provide much information on that subject.

The policy dimensions are scope, form, and value orientations. The first refers to the degree of policy inclusiveness. Is there a country-wide approach to the issue, expressed at various levels, or is national purpose involved selectively through a few critical levers with far-reaching impact (i.e., strategic), or merely episodic and fragmentary? The second expresses the form of action, the mechanism, which is mainly relied upon to attain

TABLE 2

Summary Overview: Land Policies of the Traditional Three

Habitat Land Issues

Countries	Use			Cost			Ownership		
United Kingdom	c	r	rm	c	f	rm	s	d	rm
United States	c	r	e	l	r	q	l	r	e
France	s	d	rm	s	d	rm	s	d	rm

Policy dimensions

Scope:	c	comprehensive
	s	strategic
	l	limited
Form:	r	regulatory
	d	direct action
	f	fiscal
Value orientation:	q	status quo
	e	experimental
	rm	reform

policy aims. Does the country rely primarily upon legislation which regulates the conduct of major actors, directly intervene to stop something or create something, or use the sanction of the dollar or the pound, etc.? The third dimension is value orientation, an indicator of the basic posture of the country vis-à-vis social change. Does the policy area exhibit a glacial immobility? Are there signs of only occasional innovative initiative, or is the country in question wholly committed to new and unorthodox ways of dealing with problems?

The summary overview identifies each country in terms of issues and policy dimensions. The striking feature of the comparison is the laissez-faire approach of the United States. It is a country which has acquired some deserved notoriety for the vigour of its experimentation, from great regional planning initiatives like the Tennessee Valley Authority to new concepts of land tenure such as the scenic, access, and resource management easements of Wisconsin. But overall one is left with the impression from the material submitted to Habitat that there is little forward movement on land issues in basic terms. The leadership from the centre, Washington, has been subtle and, one suspects, erratic since it depends on the rise and fall of policy commitment and budgetary support for pro-

1. Two of the most critical problems of society today, made increasingly urgent by the rapid rise in the world's population, are the deterioration of the conditions in which people live and work and the appropriate, socially acceptable use of land.

2. There are over three and a half billion people unevenly distributed over the world's habitable areas. The quality of their lives is to a major extent influenced by patterns of population growth, density, and land use.

3. The balance between the earth's peoples and the earth's ability to support them is a priority matter for global concern and action.

4. Despite progress in road development over the past decade, the road system in India has fallen far short of the growing requirements of traffic.

5. Singapore's land area is only 224 square miles, and rapid economic growth is creating problems of housing, transportation, and industrial location for its population, which will number 4 million by 1990.

6. Rising with the morning sun to face the day promises nothing but hopelessness to the street-people of Calcutta.

7. Singapore's 17,000-acre Jurong Industrial Estate includes seventy factories, which employ 10,000 workers.

8. Toa Payoh Housing Estate on the northern outskirts of the city is the largest of Singapore's satellite towns and home to more than 180,000 people.

grammes that are supposed to encourage state and local action. Philosophies, institutions, processes, enduring relationships are not being built, and the natural centrifugal forces of a very large country take over.

American policy has been especially somnambulant on the cost and ownership issues. Action on land values appears to be a blank. American adherence to a privatist posture on the issue of land ownership is clearly demonstrated by the new community programme. "Captains of Industry" like James W. Rouse, the highly innovative head of the company that built Columbia, Maryland, have testified before Congress in the most vivid terms concerning the unworkability of the reliance of the Urban Growth and New Communities Act, 1965-70, upon the private assembly of large sites.[34] Without public land assembly, the heating up of real estate markets in response to developers' manoeuvres and the consequent price escalation which becomes a built-in capital burden cannot be escaped. It is perhaps significant that in the same period that the American programme ground to a halt — in January 1975 HUD imposed "a moratorium on issuing any new commitments under the program" — the five new towns in the Paris regions, using the facilities of ZAD, were on target. Between 1968 and 1975 they were successful in deflecting a growth of close to half a million people away from the metropolitan core.[35]

In contrast to the American approach, which reflects a difference in value systems, geographic scale, and perhaps the constraints of a federal structure of government, British and French land policy is highly activist. Each attempts to percolate national policy down through a hierarchical planning structure, extending from the national capital to the parish pump. Each, in recent years, has moved towards a degree of regional decentralization and the use of positive instruments, economic and urban development, to shape the human settlement pattern directly. The French, more than the British, have a thoroughgoing strategy — Paris, counter-magnets, middle size cities, country towns — which shapes the deployment of public and private development resources.

Both the United Kingdom and France are preoccupied with the cost and ownership issues. Britain's recent comprehensive initiative to resolve these issues through the Community Land Act, 1975, is remarkable in the light of the numerous abortive attempts by former British governments. Policy-makers must this time be taking account of a feature which was absent from previous programmes, namely the local assembly on a large scale of land reserves at a price level marginally above existing use value. With sufficient development land available, the withholding of private land in response to a hefty plus value tax presumably will be less of a threat.

The French approach to these closely related issues is strongly strategic, involves direct intervention in the land market, and, after fifteen years of operation, represents a major commitment to reform. Although like that of the British, French policy is concerned with facilitating the acquisition of land for broad public purposes at non-punitive costs which exclude the publicly-induced betterment value, it does not, like the British policy, attempt to tax away all unearned increments. As one commentator has observed: "taxation of general betterment . . . would likely be vigorously resisted by French taxpayers."[36] Still, land policy in France is of great interest for dynamic urbanized countries because of the success attained by the public sector in implementing essential programmes without being held for ransom by the land market.

3

SOME COMMONWEALTH COUNTRIES AND WEST EUROPEAN SOCIAL DEMOCRACIES

OVERVIEW

A number of broad policy patterns emerge from a comparative look at the other two groups of countries, as shown in Table 3. One is impressed in the selected Commonwealth group by a preoccupation with land ownership. This factor in each of the three countries has become the key to coping effectively with all other land-related issues associated with urbanization. As Table 3 indicates, there is an overriding land-use planning process, particularly strong in Singapore and weakest in India, and specific measures are addressed to the "plus value" issue, but land tenure in all its ramifications is considered the determining factor. Ironically, while this policy focus, as a concept, has had its clearest articulation in Australia, as a practice it is observed least in that country.

This emphasis is shared most positively in the European countries under review by Sweden. "A gradual transfer of influence over land from the individual land owners to the community at large" is the way Sweden interpreted its land policy to the Habitat conference.[1] While Denmark and The Netherlands also give some attention to this factor, their greatest policy exertions are reserved for national-scale influence on land-use and settlement patterns. Their chosen mechanisms for this purpose are, however, decidedly different. The relative inattention to the price of land as a policy concern, particularly in The Netherlands, has taken its toll (at least until the mid-seventies) in a rising spiral of housing costs.[2]

It becomes apparent as comparative policy analysis proceeds that certain motifs recur, such as statutory-based regulation of land use at the central government or state (province) level. This makes all the more interesting those initiatives which are unique, which reflect the indelible stamp of a country's distinctive traditions and world view. While direct inferences from one country's experience to another's are dubious, the fascination with the international policy kaleidoscope remains because the precipitating problems, such as land abuse and price escalation, are

TABLE 3

Summary Overview: Land Policies, Selected Commonwealth
and Western European Countries

Habitat Land Issues

Countries	Use			Cost			Ownership		
Australia	c	r	e	l	d	e	s	r	e
India	l	r	e	l	d	rm	c	d	rm
Singapore	c	r	rm	c	r	rm	c	d	rm
Denmark	c	r	rm	l	r	q	c	r	q
The Netherlands	c	d	rm	l	r	q	c	d	rm
Sweden	s	r	rm	s	f	rm	c	d	rm

Policy dimensions

Scope:	c	comprehensive
	s	strategic
	l	limited
Form:	r	regulatory
	d	direct action
	f	fiscal
Value orientation:	q	status quo
	e	experimental
	rm	reform

suffered by all. It is with this perspective that I will now focus on the land policy highlights of the remaining countries under review.

AUSTRALIA:

A FRONTAL ATTACK ON LAND PRICE INFLATION IN SOUTH AUSTRALIA,
AT A TIME OF NATIONAL DEBATE AND EXPERIMENT ON LAND POLICIES

The state of South Australia, moved by the spectre of spiralling land prices in metropolitan Adelaide, established a Land Commission and Land Price Control Unit (Urban Land [Price Control] Act, November 29, 1973) as co-ordinated instruments to "stabilise the price of urban land," "secure land value increments resulting from the conversion of land to urban use for the community," and "achieve comprehensive and orderly urban development." The Commission, funded mainly by central government loan funds, assembled within two years over 10,600 acres (two-thirds for urban development, one-third for open space) in the urban fringe of Adelaide, and undertook the servicing of several thousand lots, which were delivered at prices dramatically below the prevailing market level. In a relatively few years, the Commission has become the dominant influence on the metropolitan land market, and is able to claim, with some conviction, that "the speculative element previously involved in the market for such land with consequential price effects will no longer apply." This claim is reinforced by selective price controls on vacant allotments (less than one-fifth of a hectare) of residential land both within the built-up area and on the fringe of Adelaide.[3]

The initiatives in South Australia appear to be in the forefront of a fundamental reappraisal of land policy initiated by two national enquiries in the early seventies, on the subjects of land tenure and the "national estate." While the recommendations of the Commission of Enquiry on Land Tenure are as contentious as they are far-reaching, its study process and report will endure as a momentous event in the development of Australian land policy. Much that flows from it in specific terms, from a national land-use council to the public appropriation of development rights, has its source in this philosophy:

Formulation of a land policy is not only important for the purposes of deter-mining appropriate forms of land tenure, but is an essential link in a chain of policies directed towards protecting the natural environment, improving the quality of urban life, facilitating economic management and controlling the forces of growth. In its most general sense, a national land policy may be seen as a means of responding appropriately to the pressure of population growth and development, especially in urban areas. The keystone of govern-ment policy must be a recognition that land is both a basic national resource of limited or finite extent and a necessity of life for all Australians.[4]

While this formulation, not surprisingly, has not found universal acclaim in the country's political debate, the closely related concept of national estate has been acted on by the present government. "The national estate," as defined by a recent act, "consists of those places, being com-ponents of the natural environment of Australia or the cultural environ-ment of Australia, that have aesthetic, historic, scientific or social signifi-cance or other special value for future generations as well as for the present community." The setting up of the Australian Heritage Commis-sion to protect, restore, and conserve the national estate has been heralded as "a revolution in social consciousness."[5]

INDIA:
LIMITS ESTABLISHED TO THE HOLDING OF VACANT LAND AND THE MANDATORY SURRENDERING OF EXCESS VACANT LANDS TO THE GOVERNMENT AT CONTROLLED PRICES

India, it seems, is concerned almost equally with the impact of rapidly rising freehold land prices in metropolitan areas (for example, in Delhi; the price there increased by a multiple of ten from 1960 to 1975); and with equity, the sharing of the land. Accordingly, its statement of urban land policy includes this objective: "To prevent concentration of land ownership in a few private hands and safeguard the interest of the poor and under-privileged sections of urban society."[6]

This is the background to the Urban Land (Ceiling and Regulation) Act, 1976, which, in forty-eight urban agglomerations, imposes ceilings on both the private holding of vacant land and on the ground floor area of dwellings and also regulates private property transactions. Details indicating the thrust of the legislation are the application of the act to all private, corporate, or institutional owners; the quite modest allowable holdings, ranging from 500 square metres in the largest places (metropolitan Delhi, Bombay, Calcutta, and Madras), to 2,000 square metres in urban agglomerations with a population between 200,000 and 300,000; the calculation of "excess holdings" by aggregating individual ownerships held in all urban agglomerations; and the limiting of compensation from the public purse to strictly non-inflated levels. For example, the amount allowable for non-income-bearing property in Delhi, rs. 10 per square metre, is at about what the level was "in a typical middle class residential locality" in 1956.[7]

The expectation is that the monitoring and approval of property transfers will preclude "speculative transactions" and that the assembly of excess lands by the government will dramatically enhance its capability to influence the location of industry and the general settlement pattern.

SINGAPORE:
CLOSE INTEGRATION OF PLANNING, HOUSING, INCREMENT TAXATION AND LAND ACQUISITION

Public policy in Singapore is centrally concerned with the allocation of scarce space within a highly restricted land base to fiercely competing needs, including a mammoth public housing programme, without incurring serious diseconomies. As a result, the Master Plan for Singapore and its zoning instrument are pivotal as an allocative mechanism which interacts with a number of checks and balances. For example, the Plan, first approved in 1958, has served to designate and reserve sufficient land for the Housing and Development Board to construct between 1960 and

1975 approximately a quarter of a million dwelling units, "one of the highest rates of housing in the world" according to a World Bank study. To acquire this building space, much of it privately held, the government found it necessary to introduce the Land Acquisition Act, 1966. This act authorized public purchase of private land for general urban development on a compulsory basis at a compensation value which discounts increments arising out of public improvements on the land and surroundings in the preceding seven years, and then later at a price pegged at the 1973 level.[8]

Any land value increments which might accrue as a result of approved changes in the zoning are soaked up by development charges, one on density increases and another on land use changes. Land cannot be held indefinitely, perhaps with speculative intent; planning permission for public land sold or leased or for private land transfers and development does not exceed two years.[9]

The Singapore system restrained land prices until 1972, when they appeared to break loose. This has been attributed to several factors: the acquisition of land in "more favourable locations"; the reluctance to invoke the expropriation power; and the rising surge of economic activity and housing demand up to the early seventies. The government's response was to reinforce the planning-housing-land acquisition instruments and the active development role of the public sector. On balance, the independent judgment is rendered that "advanced land acquisition and development policies in Singapore" have succeeded in "appropriating betterment for social use."[10]

DENMARK:
NATIONAL LEVEL ACTION TO CONTROL THE CONVERSION
OF AGRICULTURAL LAND TO URBAN PURPOSES

Since 1969 the use of land in Denmark has been controlled by the Urban and Rural Zones Act. The Danish approach is deceptively simple, and yet appears to be very effective. Commencing from the premise that the relationship of the city to the open country is from a *national* point of view, the critical land-use issue, the act defines the urban/rural fence, and sets up very explicit rules for moving it.

Urban zones are based on the areas designated in the regional plans prepared by the county councils and the Greater Copenhagen Council and approved by the Minister of the Environment. "To ensure uninterrupted development and in particular to prevent speculation in land prices, Denmark's zoning policy requires that planners at all times include sufficient land in urban zones to meet the needs of future years." The remaining areas are limited districts set aside for "holiday housing," and rural zones, making up 95 per cent of the total, which are confined to agriculture, forestry, and fisheries.[11]

From the perspective of planning law it is interesting to note that the Danish legislation provides for compensation to landowners only under precisely and quite narrowly defined conditions: "Where a landowner on location in a rural zone in 1970 was precluded from making economically reasonable and adequate use of his property corresponding to the actual use of neighbouring properties," and "only where an application was submitted not later than six months after the entry into force of the act on January 1, 1970." On this point the National Report observes, sagely: "There is political agreement on the need for public control of land use, and it is a political issue to what extent compensation should be made to individual landowners for their loss."[12]

Within the expansive framework of the national zoning plan, the land-use pattern is progressively refined by the National Planning Committee, a supervisory, long-range planning group, the regional plans, and the conservation plans. The latter are evolved at the county level under the authority of the Nature Conservation Act, 1969, and are noteworthy for a broad mandate — scientific, educational, historical, and recreational concerns — and for the array of implementing instruments available: easements, protective zones, and special approval systems for major infrastructure in the countryside.[13]

THE NETHERLANDS:
NATIONAL ACTION TO SHAPE THE LAND-USE AND
SETTLEMENT PATTERN OF THE COUNTRY

In The Netherlands, the constraint of space makes land policy inseparable from national settlement policy. While at the national level there is no legally binding plan, there is a government policy that reverberates through the country's multi-tiered planning system. "The government aims to ensure a coherent physical planning policy at central government level and to this end the Physical Planning Act states that all measures and plans relevant to the policy must be referred to a central coordinating body (The National Planning Committee)."[14]

The concept that has assumed dominance over the past two decades is known as "clustered deconcentration," to suggest the consolidation and stabilization of existing central cities, with growth not exceeding natural increase and the channeling of overflow population to selected "growth centres." Spatially this takes the form of a "green core" at the heart of "Randstad Holland," the network consisting of Rotterdam-The Hague-Leiden-Amsterdam and Utrecht, and a number of medium-sized centres, some beyond, some within the ring. Two of these are new towns, Zoetermeer, east of The Hague, and Almere, in the new polder east of Amsterdam. The anticipated benefits of this settlement pattern are *environmental*: to ease pressure on the big cities and to maintain recreational areas; *economic*: to attain greater inter-regional equity and to sustain productive farmland; and *communal*: to "prevent the development of a megalopolis which would not permit the conservation of the characteristic identity of the different cities."[15]

The Dutch planning system has a highly evolved planning and regulatory machinery from regional plans (provincial) to structural and allocative plans (municipal). To implement the national settlement policy these are supplemented by positive measures such as subventions to stimulate employment in "growth centres" and the whole apparatus, technical and financial, of new town building which the Dutch have developed to a high art in half a century of creating polder communities.

A critique of this policy was undertaken by F. Grunfeld on behalf of the Habitat conference, and he found it, in some respects, unfulfilled. Two sets of observations are particularly revealing. One is that the population of the green core has, after fifteen years of stability (1946-60), commenced a counter-policy trend, rising from 4.3 per cent of its district in 1960 to 5.2 per cent in 1970 and 5.8 per cent in 1974. The other is that the growth centres, experiencing difficulties associated with initially high infrastructure costs, attracted less overspill population than suburban communities. High capital costs raised the prices of building sites, which led to multi-storey apartments which placed the growth centres at a competitive disadvantage. "So while the 'competing' smaller communities were able to offer at the same or even at a lower price one-family row-houses ... the should-be-growth centres only developed ... with evident difficulties.[16]

While Grunfeld usefully identifies the pitfalls of the complex land settlement policy of The Netherlands, some of his data indicate that the basic aim of depressurizing the Ranstad has had a measure of success. Population is down from 47.6 per cent of the national total in 1960 to 45.6 per cent in 1974, the number of people living in the largest places is significantly lower, and the share of employment remained level for about a decade.

SWEDEN:

MUNICIPAL LAND OWNERSHIP, BACKED UP BY NATIONAL LAWS AND
FUNDING, AS THE KEY TO ATTAINING ENVIRONMENTAL GOALS,
AND RELYING ON A STRONG LAND ETHIC

One of the interesting things about land policy in Sweden is that the urban aspects of that policy rest on principles and concepts that have evolved, since the turn of the last century, out of a concern for the public stewardship of natural resources. In 1974, a complex history of forest management legislation culminated in an act which established, unequivocally, that "land ownership is in no way absolute and may only be permitted within the limits fixed by legislative bodies in the country, one of the aims being to ensure the right type of use and management for land in the long term and in the interests of the entire nation."[17]

Against the background of this kind of social climate, municipalities in Sweden have a principal role in the management of urban growth. Stockholm's legendary achievements in this regard are representative of the general approach. As indicated in a Swedish report to Habitat concerning land policy, the national government has fostered this role by:

1　a decree (1967) requesting local authorities to create 10-year land banks for urban expansion;
2　[providing] a state loan fund for municipal land purchases (1968);
3　authorizing land expropriation by local authorities, with controls over compensation values (1949);
4　the "preemption prerogative" — a statutory requirement that municipalities be notified of private property transactions and be given first claim on the land in question during a waiting period of three months (1968);
5　the policy that eligibility for state housing loans to developers/builders depends on the purchase or lease of municipal land. Since about 90% of all residential construction is at least partially financed by state loans, this condition substantially strengthens the muncipal control over land use (1975).[18]

The Swedish report concludes as follows: "The trend in Sweden has revealed that important public goals can be achieved by a gradual shift in the implications of land ownership ... Each change has been motivated by a wish to achieve specific goals. Active land policy on the part of the community has thus been one of the means employed to achieve these ends, and not an end in itself."[19] Land policy is central in the country's development strategy. Independent judgment identifies public ownership of land as the supreme influence on the pattern of urban expansion in Sweden.[20]

4

CONCLUSIONS

A number of observations emerge from the foregoing review of urban land policies in nine countries. The first, and most striking, is the great variety of policy responses. There is a rich and diversified pluralism which in itself is a stimulus to policy thinking. Canada, in its report to Habitat, expressed concern about sprawl, the wasteful and uneconomic use of land on the urban fringe. Could this problem be overcome by the Canadian provinces borrowing preferential assessments from the American states, some form of development zoning from France, and the land commission approach of South Australia; and by the federal government, through C.M.H.C., reinforcing these efforts by attaching land ownership and price criteria to its loans, along the lines of the Swedish practice? Finding the right answers to this kind of conjecture lies along the tough path of evaluative policy research. Habitat has been a vehicle for broadening our view of both problems and policy options, thereby making policy enquiry eminently richer in its potential.

A second observation is that there is a strong correlation between the severity of land issues and the prominence of comprehensive national level action. The United Kingdom, Singapore, Denmark and The Netherlands illustrate this correlation. This unremarkable conclusion holds a special interest for a country like Canada, where the land constraints are not yet so overwhelming. The policy experience of those countries can be viewed as an extremely instructive laboratory. By learning the lessons of a variety of approaches — Britain's difficulties with the increment tax, for example — Canada can avoid the crisis syndrome in policy-making: the hasty contrivance of measures followed by a series of perverse and counter-productive reverberations.

A third and final observation is that the countries closest to Canada, with the exception of the United States, but including large, multi-governmental states like Australia and India, all display greater concern with land problems — urban land and the urban/rural relationships —

31

than does official Canada. What is at issue is the quality of leadership on problems that assume national dimensions. For example, the fate (use, cost, ownership, development) of the 85,000 square miles that constitute the fringe lands of Canadian towns and cities which in the next quarter century will be the prime habitat for new residential communities, for food production (apart from staple grains), recreation, and water.[1]

I am aware of backroom Ottawa discussion on land in Urban Affairs and Environment and have heard whispers about a national land-use policy, but the failure of these activities to surface in any tangible way must be cause for the deepest concern. Canada is better prepared than most countries through its land capability inventory (with all its lack of refinement) for the formulation of sound national targets. Some of the experience cited, such as Australia's central government support of state-level land commissions, and effective municipal action in Sweden backed up by national legislation, provides some clues to how such targets may be translated into action, while respecting jurisdictional prerogatives.

This international review of land policy whets the appetite for deeper and broader investigation. The analysis of each set of policies turns up some new insight, some intriguing nuance. And yet policy analysis by its very nature implies that at some point a moratorium on studies must be called, and the implications of new knowledge must be assessed.

To translate the material in this study to a policy document of direct application to the land dilemmas faced in Canada would require an in-depth treatment of Canadian conditions in a number of respects. Canadian public policies and programmes, in major jurisdictional spheres, would have to be clarified. The successes and failures of such initiatives would have to be evaluated. And cross-cultural/political analysis would have to be undertaken to identify those aspects of the international pool of experience that have the greatest relevance for Canada.[2]

NOTES

CHAPTER I: SCOPE OF LAND POLICY CONCERNS

1 Report of the Third Committee Habitat Vancouver A/CONF. 70/11, June 8, 1976, introduction to the recommendations for national action on land; press release, June 11, 1976, Habitat, Vancouver, HE/V/77, p. 1.

2 *Ibid.*, Report of the Third Committee, Recommendations D.1 to D.7.

3 Committee 3, June 2, 1976, a.m., observer discussion notes.

4 Peter Nicholson, "The Habitat '76 Conference: A Personal Assessment," *Habitat*, XIX, 3/4 (1976).

5 *A Statement of Habitat*, The Canadian Real Estate Association, Vancouver, June 1976.

6 *C.A.S.E. News Magazine*, Habitat Issue, IV, 2 (1976), p. 22; Brief Submitted by the Students of Inter-Provincial Seminar of the United Nations, Vancouver, June 7, 1976, recommendation 5 on land use.

7 *Human Settlement in Canada* (Ottawa: Ministry of State for Urban Affairs, 1976), pp. 98, 99.

8 Committee 3, June 3, 1976, a.m., observer notes. "Lesotho's Explanation Helps Them All," *Jericho*, June 4, 1976, p. 2.

CHAPTER 2: DOMINANT INFLUENCES: THE TRADITIONAL THREE

1 United Kingdom National Report, Habitat, Vancouver, 1976, p. 19; *An Outline of Planning in the United Kingdom*, Habitat (Vancouver: Department of the Environment, 1976), p. 60.

2 *Ibid., Outline of Planning*, pp. 63, 64.

3 *The Role of Government in New Urban Developments in the United Kingdom* (Vancouver: Department of the Environment, 1976), par. 11.

4 *Ibid.*, par. 3.

5 *Ibid.*, pars. 24-26, 30. Recaptured development values actually go to a central body, the New Towns Commission, responsible for the overall supervision and financing of new town development.

6 U.K. National Report, pp. 16, 17.

⁷ *Ibid.*, Community Land Scheme, par. 12.

⁸ Orville F. Grimes, *Urban Land and Public Policy: Social Appropriation of Betterment*, Bank Staff Working Paper 179 (Washington, D.C.: International Bank for Reconstruction and Development, May 1974), pp. 21-25.

⁹ G. Max Neutze, *The Price of Land and Land Use Planning* (Paris: O.E.C.D., 1973), pp. 90, 91.

¹⁰ *Outline of Planning*, p. 60.

¹¹ *Ibid.*, pp. 68, 69; *Audio-Visual Catalogue*, Habitat, Vancouver, 1976. Note U.K. film UK 012 "The Waste of Waste Land," p. 48.

¹² U.S.A. National Report, State Growth Management, Habitat, Vancouver, 1976, p. 26.

¹³ U.S.A. National Report, Changing Issues for National Growth, Habitat, Vancouver, 1976, pp. 127-29.

¹⁴ *Ibid.*, p. 128.

¹⁵ The issue, however, is a lively public concern, currently expressed in on-going public or private commissions and processes in about twenty-five states.

¹⁶ Changing Issues, pp. 131-32; State Growth Management, pp. 23, 26.

¹⁷ Changing Issues for National Growth, p. 131.

¹⁸ State Growth Management, p. 26.

¹⁹ *Ibid.*

²⁰ *Ibid.*, pp. 134, 135.

²¹ *Ibid.*, pp. 135, 136.

²² U.S.A. National Report, Summary Evaluation Research, Habitat, Vancouver, 1976, pp. 5, 8; *ibid.*, pp. 128, 131, 132.

²³ Summary Evaluation Research, p. 1.

²⁴ *Ibid.*, pp. 7, 8.

²⁵ *Ibid.*, p. 2.

²⁶ France National Report, Habitat, Vancouver, 1976, pp. 15-17, 50-52.

²⁷ C. R. Bryant and L. G. R. Martin, "Public Land Assembly and Land Price Monitoring: The Case of the ZAD in the Paris Region," *Plan Canada*, 6/3, 4 Sept./Dec. 1976, pp. 178, 179.

²⁸ *Ibid.*, pp. 179-80; Grimes, *Urban Land and Public Policy*, p. 30. There was an earlier mechanism, started in 1958, known as Zone d'Urbanisation en Priorité (ZUP: Zone of Priority Development). This operated like ZAD but on a four-year basis, with an optional extension of two years. It has been virtually replaced by the combined operation of ZAD and ZAC. Grimes, p. 29; Bryant and Martin, "Public Land Assembly . . . ," p. 179.

²⁹ Bryant and Martin, "Public Land Assembly . . . ," pp. 179, 181, 182, 185.

[30] *Ibid.*, p. 187.

[31] *Ibid.*, pp. 180, 181.

[32] Grimes, *Urban Land and Public Policy*, pp. 30, 31.

[33] Bryant and Martin, "Public Land Assembly . . . ," pp. 188, 189.

[34] James W. Rouse, "The City of Columbia, Maryland," in *Taming Megalopolis*, II, H. Wentworth Eldredge, editor (New York: Doubleday, 1967), pp. 838-48.

[35] U.S.A. National Report, Changing Issues for National Growth, p. 135; Bryant and Martin, "Public Land Assembly . . . ," p. 185.

[36] Grimes, *Urban Land and Public Policy*, p. 30.

CHAPTER 3: SOME COMMONWEALTH COUNTRIES AND WEST EUROPEAN
SOCIAL DEMOCRACIES

[1] Peter Heimburger, *Land Policy in Sweden*, Habitat, Vancouver (Stockholm: Ministry of Housing and Physical Planning, 1976), p. 4.

[2] G. Max Neutze, *The Price of Land and Land Use Planning* (Paris: O.E.C.D., 1973), pp. 59, 60.

[3] "Controlling the Price of Land for Development," Government of South Australia, Australia National Report, Habitat, Vancouver, 1976, p. 71.

[4] *Report of the Commission of Inquiry into Land Tenure*, Final Report (Canberra: Government of Australia, February 1976), p. 11.

[5] Len Webb and Judith Wright-McKinney, "Concept of the National Estate," Australia National Report, Habitat, Vancouver, 1976, pp. 273, 277.

[6] India National Report, Habitat, Vancouver, 1976, p. 50.

[7] *Socialisation of Urban Land* (New Delhi: Ministry of Works and Housing, Government of India, 1975), pp. 4, 6.

[8] Singapore National Report, Habitat, Vancouver, 1976, pp. 7, 8, 10; Grimes, *Urban Land and Public Policy*, pp. 46, 47.

[9] *Ibid.*, Grimes, p. 43; Singapore National Report, p. 8.

[10] Grimes, *Urban Land and Public Policy*, pp. 47, 48.

[11] Denmark National Report, Habitat, Vancouver, 1976, pp. 8, 9.

[12] *Ibid.*, pp. 9, 10.

[13] *Ibid.*, pp. 10, 11.

[14] The Netherlands National Report, Habitat, Vancouver, 1976, p. 7.

[15] F. Grunfeld, *National and Regional Planning: A Critical Survey of Some Experiences in The Netherlands*, Habitat, Vancouver, 1976, pp. 5-7.

[16] *Ibid.*, pp. 7, 10, 11, 15.

[17] Heimburger, *Land Policy in Sweden*, pp. 16, 17.

[18] *Ibid.*, pp. 28, 29, 31, 36, 37.

[19] *Ibid.*, p. 44.

[20] Neutze, *The Price of Land and Land Use Planning*, pp. 74, 75.

CHAPTER 4: CONCLUSION

[1] L. O. Gertler and R. W. Crowley, *Changing Canadian Cities: The Next Twenty-Five Years* (Toronto: McClelland and Stewart, 1977), pp. 267-99, 444.

[2] L. S. Bourne, *Urban Systems: Strategies for Regulation* (Oxford: Clarendon Press, 1975). Note discussions of factors in cross-national comparisons, pp. 5-9, and Chapters 6 and 7.

APPENDIX

Habitat Recommendations for National Action on Land

D *Land* (Agenda item 10 (d))

Preamble

1 Land, because of its unique nature and the crucial role it plays in human settlements, cannot be treated as an ordinary asset, controlled by individuals and subject to the pressures and inefficiencies of the market. Private land ownership is also a principal instrument of accumulation and concentration of wealth and therefore contributes to social injustice; if unchecked, it may become a major obstacle in the planning and implementation of development schemes. Social justice, urban renewal and development, the provision of decent dwellings and healthy conditions for the people can only be achieved if land is used in the interests of society as a whole.

2 Instead, the pattern of land use should be determined by the long-term interests of the community, especially since decisions on location of activities and therefore of specific land uses have a long-lasting effect on the pattern and structure of human settlements. Land is also a primary element of the natural and man-made environment and a crucial link in an often delicate balance. Public control of land use is therefore indispensable to its protection as an asset and the achievement of the long-term objectives of human settlement policies and strategies.

3 To exercise such control effectively, public authorities require detailed knowledge of the current patterns of use and tenure of land; appropriate legislation defining the boundaries of individual rights and public interest; and suitable instruments for assessing the value of land and transferring to the community, *inter alia* through taxation, the unearned increment resulting from changes in use, or public investment or decisions, or due to the general growth of the community.

4 Above all, Governments must have the political will to evolve and implement innovative and adequate urban and rural land policies, as a cornerstone of their efforts to improve the quality of life in human settlements.

Recommendation D.1

Land resource management

(a) Land is one of the most valuable natural resources and it must be used rationally. Public ownership or effective control of land in the public interest is the single most important means of improving the capacity of human settlements to absorb changes and movements in population, modifying their internal structure and achieving a more equitable distribution of the benefits of development whilst assuring that environmental impacts are considered.

(b) LAND IS A SCARCE RESOURCE WHOSE MANAGEMENT SHOULD BE SUBJECT TO PUBLIC SURVEILLANCE OR CONTROL IN THE INTEREST OF THE NATION.

(c) *This applies in particular to land required for:*

(i) the extension and improvement of existing settlements, the development of new ones and, in general, the achievement of a more efficient network of human settlements;

(ii) the implementation of programmes of urban renewal and land-assembly schemes;

(iii) the provisions of public shelter, infrastructure and services;

(iv) the preservation and improvement of valuable components of the man-made environment, such as historic sites and monuments and other areas of unique and aesthetic social and cultural value;

(v) the protection and enhancement of the natural environment especially in sensitive areas of special geographic and ecological significance such as coastal regions and other areas subject to the impact of development, recreation and tourism activities.

(d) Land is a natural resource fundamental to the economic, social and political development of peoples and therefore Governments must maintain full jurisdiction and exercise complete sovereignty over such land with a view to freely planning development of human settlements throughout the whole of the natural territory. This resource must not be the subject of restrictions imposed by foreign nations which enjoy the benefits while preventing its rational use.

(e) In all occupied territories, changes in the demographic composition, or the transfer or uprooting of the native population, and the destruction of existing human settlements in these lands and/or the establishment of new settlements for intruders, is inadmissible. The heritage and national identity must be protected. Any policies that violate these principles must be condemned.

Recommendation D.2

Control of land use changes

(a) Agricultural land, particularly on the periphery of urban areas, is an important national resource; without public control land is a prey to speculation and urban encroachment.

(b) CHANGE IN THE USE OF LAND, ESPECIALLY FROM AGRICULTURAL TO URBAN, SHOULD BE SUBJECT TO PUBLIC CONTROL AND REGULATION.

(c) *Such control may be exercised through:*

(i) zoning and land-use planning as a basic instrument of land policy in general and of control of land-use changes in particular;

(ii) direct intervention, e.g. the creation of land reserves and land banks, purchase, compensated expropriation and/or pre-emption, acquisition of development rights, conditioned leasing of public and communal land, formation of public and mixed development enterprises;

(iii) legal controls, e.g. compulsory registration, changes in administrative boundaries, development building and local permits, assembly and replotting;

(iv) fiscal controls, e.g. property taxes, tax penalties and tax incentives;

(v) a planned co-ordination between orderly urban development and the promotion and location of new developments, preserving agricultural land.

Recommendation D.3

Recapturing plus value

(a) Excessive profits resulting from the increase in land value due to development and change in use are one of the principal causes of the concentration of wealth in private hands. Taxation should not be seen only as a source of revenue for the community but also as a powerful tool to encourage development of desirable locations, to exercise a controlling effect on the land market and to redistribute to the public at large the benefits of the unearned increase in land values.

(b) THE UNEARNED INCREMENT RESULTING FROM THE RISE IN LAND VALUES RESULTING FROM CHANGE IN USE OF LAND, FROM PUBLIC INVESTMENT OR DECISION OR DUE TO THE GENERAL GROWTH OF THE COMMUNITY MUST BE SUBJECT TO APPROPRIATE RECAPTURE BY PUBLIC BODIES (THE COMMUNITY), UNLESS THE SITUATION CALLS FOR OTHER ADDITIONAL MEASURES SUCH AS NEW PATTERNS OF OWNERSHIP, THE GENERAL ACQUISITION OF LAND BY PUBLIC BODIES.

(c) *Specific ways and means include:*

(i) levying of appropriate taxes, e.g. capital gains taxes, land taxes and betterment charges, and particularly taxes on unused or under-utilized land;

(ii) periodic and frequent assessment of land values in and around cities, and determination of the rise in such values relative to the general level of prices;

(iii) instituting development charges or permit fees and specifying the time-limit within which construction must start;

(iv) adopting pricing and compensation policies relating to value of land prevailing at a specified time, rather than its commercial value at the time of acquisition by public authorities;

- (v) leasing of publicly owned land in such a way that future increment which is not due to the efforts by the new user is kept by the community;
- (vi) assessment of land suitable for agricultural use which is in proximity of cities mainly at agricultural values.

Recommendation D.4

Public ownership

- (a) Public ownership of land cannot be an end in itself; it is justified in so far as it is exercised in favour of the common good rather than to protect the interests of the already privileged.
- (b) PUBLIC OWNERSHIP, TRANSITIONAL OR PERMANENT, SHOULD BE USED, WHEREVER APPROPRIATE, TO SECURE AND CONTROL AREAS OF URBAN EXPANSION AND PROTECTION; AND TO IMPLEMENT URBAN AND RURAL LAND REFORM PROCESSES, AND SUPPLY SERVICED LAND AT PRICE LEVELS WHICH CAN SECURE SOCIALLY ACCEPTABLE PATTERNS OF DEVELOPMENT.
- (c) *Special consideration should be given to:*
- (i) measures outlined in Recommendations D.2 and D.3 above;
- (ii) active public participation in land development;
- (iii) rational distribution of powers among various levels of government, including communal and local authorities, and an adequate system of financial support for land policy.

Recommendation D.5

Patterns of ownership

- (a) Many countries are undergoing a process of profound social transformation; a review and restructuring of the entire system of ownership rights is, in the majority of cases, essential to the accomplishment of new national objectives.
- (b) PAST PATTERNS OF OWNERSHIP RIGHTS SHOULD BE TRANSFORMED TO MATCH THE CHANGING NEEDS OF SOCIETY AND BE COLLECTIVELY BENEFICIAL.
- (c) *Special attention should be paid to:*
- (i) redefinition of legal ownership including the rights of women and disadvantaged groups and usage rights for a variety of purposes;
- (ii) promoting land reform measures to bring ownership rights into conformity with the present and future needs of society;
- (iii) clear definition of public objectives and private ownership rights and duties which may vary with time and place;
- (iv) transitional arrangements to change ownership from traditional and customary patterns to new systems, especially in connection with communal lands, whenever such patterns are no longer appropriate;

(v) methods for the separation of land ownership rights from development rights, the latter to be entrusted to a public authority;

(vi) adoption of policies for long-term leasing of land;

(vii) the land rights of indigenous peoples so that their cultural and historical heritage is preserved.

Recommendation D.6

Increase in usable land

(a) In view of the limited availability of land for human settlements and the need to prevent the continuing loss of valuable natural areas due to erosion, urban encroachment and other causes, efforts to conserve and reclaim land for both agriculture and settlements without upsetting the ecological balance are imperative.

(b) THE SUPPLY OF USABLE LAND SHOULD BE MAINTAINED BY ALL APPROPRIATE METHODS INCLUDING SOIL CONSERVATION, CONTROL OF DESERTIFICATION AND SALINATION, PREVENTION OF POLLUTION, AND USE OF LAND CAPABILITY ANALYSIS AND INCREASED BY LONG-TERM PROGRAMMES OF LAND RECLAMATION AND PRESERVATION.

(c) *Special attention should be paid to:*

(i) land-fill, especially by using solid wastes in close proximity to human settlements, but without detriment to environment and geological conditions;

(ii) control of soil erosion, e.g. through reforestation, flood control, flood plain management, changes in cultivation patterns and methods, and controls on indiscriminate grazing;

(iii) control and reversal of desertification and salinization, and recuperation of fertile land from contamination by endemic disease;

(iv) reclamation of water-logged areas in a manner that minimizes adverse environmental effects;

(v) application of new technologies such as those related to flood control, soil conservation and stabilization and irrigation;

(vi) prevention of pollution as well as restoration of derelict or damaged land, control of fire and preservation of the environment from natural and man-made hazards;

(vii) economizing land by fixing appropriate densities in areas where land is scarce or rich in agricultural value;

(viii) proper land capability assessment programmes should be introduced at the local, regional and national levels so that land use allocation will most benefit the community; and areas suited to long-term reclamation and preservation will be identified and appropriate action taken;

(ix) incorporation of new land into settlements by provision of infrastructure;

(x) control of the location of human settlements in hazardous zones and important natural areas;

(xi) expansion of agricultural lands with proper drainage.

Recommendation D.7

Information needs

(a) Effective land use planning and control measures cannot be implemented unless the public and all levels of government have access to adequate information.

(b) COMPREHENSIVE INFORMATION ON LAND CAPABILITY, CHARACTERISTICS, TENURE, USE AND LEGISLATION SHOULD BE COLLECTED AND CONSTANTLY UP-DATED SO THAT ALL CITIZENS AND LEVELS OF GOVERNMENT CAN BE GUIDED AS TO THE MOST BENEFICIAL LAND USE ALLOCATION AND CONTROL MEASURES.

(c) *This implies:*

(i) the establishment of a comprehensive information system involving all levels of government, and accessible to the public;

(ii) topographic and cadastral surveys and assessment of land capabilities and current use, and periodic evaluations of the use of the land;

(iii) simplification and updating of procedures for collection, analysis and distribution of relevant information in an accurate and comprehensive manner;

(iv) introduction of new surveying and mapping technologies suitable to the conditions of the countries concerned;

(v) consolidation and effective use of existing or innovative legislation and instruments to implement land policies;

(vi) development and use of methods for assessing economic, social and environmental impacts from proposed projects in a form useful to the public;

(vii) consideration of land use characteristics including ecological tolerances and optimum utilization of land so as to minimize pollution, conserve energy, and protect and recover resources;

(viii) undertake the necessary studies on precautions that can be taken to safeguard life and property in case of natural disaster.

This publication is based upon work partially funded by the Ministry of State for Urban Affairs, but the views expressed are the personal views of the author and no responsibility for them should be attributed to the Ministry of State for Urban Affairs.

PHOTO CREDITS

1. Un
2. Un
3. Un
4. Un
5. Un
6. Un
7. Un
8. Un